50 Middle Eastern Delights: A Taste of Tradition

By: Kelly Johnson

Table of Contents

- Hummus with Olive Oil and Paprika
- Baba Ganoush (Smoky Eggplant Dip)
- Falafel with Tahini Sauce
- Shakshuka (Poached Eggs in Spiced Tomato Sauce)
- Manakish (Za'atar Flatbread)
- Fattoush Salad with Pomegranate Dressing
- Tabbouleh (Parsley and Bulgur Salad)
- Muhammara (Red Pepper and Walnut Dip)
- Kibbeh (Stuffed Bulgur and Meat Croquettes)
- Sfiha (Lebanese Meat Pies)
- Lamb Kofta Skewers
- Chicken Shawarma with Garlic Sauce
- Beef Kebab with Sumac Onions
- Mujadara (Lentils and Rice with Caramelized Onions)
- Koshari (Egyptian Lentil and Pasta Dish)
- Foul Medames (Fava Bean Stew)
- Stuffed Grape Leaves (Dolma)
- Makloubeh (Upside-Down Rice and Meat Dish)
- Samak Mashwi (Grilled Fish with Spices)
- Lebanese Garlic Toum Sauce
- Harira (Moroccan Chickpea Soup)
- Tahini and Date Energy Bites
- Labneh with Olive Oil and Za'atar
- Roz Bel Laban (Creamy Rice Pudding)
- Basbousa (Semolina Coconut Cake)
- Kunafa (Crispy Cheese and Syrup Dessert)
- Baklava with Pistachios and Honey
- Atayef (Stuffed Pancakes with Nuts or Cream)
- Maamoul (Date-Filled Shortbread Cookies)
- Qatayef Asafiri (Mini Pancakes with Cream)
- Halva (Sweet Sesame Paste Dessert)
- Cardamom and Saffron Rice Pudding
- Persian Love Cake with Rose Water
- Turkish Delight with Pistachios
- Pomegranate Molasses Chicken

- Bamia (Okra and Tomato Stew)
- Fasolia (White Bean and Tomato Stew)
- Moroccan Spiced Carrot Salad
- Dukkah-Crusted Roasted Vegetables
- Feta and Olive Mezze Platter
- Grilled Halloumi with Honey and Nuts
- Shish Taouk (Middle Eastern Chicken Skewers)
- Spiced Lentil Soup with Cumin and Coriander
- Batata Harra (Spicy Lebanese Potatoes)
- Warak Enab (Grape Leaves Stuffed with Rice and Meat)
- Arayes (Stuffed Pita with Spiced Meat)
- Sahlab (Warm Milk and Orchid Powder Drink)
- Rosewater Lemonade with Mint
- Turkish Coffee with Cardamom
- Mint Tea with Pine Nuts

Hummus with Olive Oil and Paprika

Ingredients:

- 1 can chickpeas, drained
- 2 tablespoons tahini
- 1 clove garlic, minced
- 1 tablespoon lemon juice
- 2 tablespoons olive oil
- ½ teaspoon salt
- ½ teaspoon cumin
- ½ teaspoon paprika (for garnish)

Instructions:

1. Blend chickpeas, tahini, garlic, lemon juice, olive oil, salt, and cumin until smooth.
2. Add water if needed for consistency.
3. Drizzle with olive oil and sprinkle with paprika before serving.

Baba Ganoush (Smoky Eggplant Dip)

Ingredients:

- 1 large eggplant
- 2 tablespoons tahini
- 1 clove garlic, minced
- 1 tablespoon lemon juice
- 1 tablespoon olive oil
- ½ teaspoon salt
- ½ teaspoon smoked paprika

Instructions:

1. Roast eggplant at 400°F (200°C) for 30–40 minutes until soft.
2. Scoop out flesh and blend with tahini, garlic, lemon juice, olive oil, and salt.
3. Drizzle with more olive oil and sprinkle with smoked paprika.

Falafel with Tahini Sauce

Ingredients:

- 1 can chickpeas, drained
- 1 small onion, chopped
- 2 cloves garlic, minced
- ¼ cup fresh parsley
- 1 teaspoon cumin
- 1 teaspoon coriander
- 2 tablespoons flour
- ½ teaspoon salt
- 1 tablespoon olive oil

Tahini Sauce:

- ¼ cup tahini
- 1 tablespoon lemon juice
- 1 clove garlic, minced
- 2 tablespoons water

Instructions:

1. Blend chickpeas, onion, garlic, parsley, cumin, coriander, flour, and salt.
2. Shape into small patties and bake at 375°F (190°C) for 20 minutes.
3. Mix tahini, lemon juice, garlic, and water for sauce.
4. Serve falafel with tahini sauce.

Shakshuka (Poached Eggs in Spiced Tomato Sauce)

Ingredients:

- 1 tablespoon olive oil
- 1 small onion, diced
- 2 cloves garlic, minced
- 1 teaspoon cumin
- ½ teaspoon paprika
- 1 can diced tomatoes
- 4 eggs
- Salt and pepper to taste
- Fresh parsley for garnish

Instructions:

1. Heat olive oil in a pan and sauté onion and garlic.
2. Add cumin, paprika, and tomatoes. Simmer for 10 minutes.
3. Make small wells in the sauce and crack eggs in.
4. Cover and cook until eggs are set.
5. Garnish with parsley and serve with bread.

Manakish (Za'atar Flatbread)

Ingredients:

- 2 cups all-purpose flour
- 1 teaspoon salt
- 1 teaspoon sugar
- 1 teaspoon yeast
- ¾ cup warm water
- 2 tablespoons olive oil
- 2 tablespoons za'atar spice mix

Instructions:

1. Mix flour, salt, sugar, and yeast in a bowl.
2. Add warm water and knead into a dough. Let rise for 1 hour.
3. Roll out and brush with olive oil, then sprinkle za'atar.
4. Bake at 400°F (200°C) for 12–15 minutes.

Fattoush Salad with Pomegranate Dressing

Ingredients:

- 2 cups chopped romaine lettuce
- ½ cucumber, diced
- ½ cup cherry tomatoes, halved
- ¼ cup radishes, sliced
- 1 small pita, toasted and crumbled
- ¼ cup pomegranate seeds
- 2 tablespoons olive oil
- 1 tablespoon pomegranate molasses
- 1 teaspoon sumac
- Salt and pepper to taste

Instructions:

1. Toss vegetables, pita, and pomegranate seeds in a bowl.
2. Whisk olive oil, pomegranate molasses, sumac, salt, and pepper.
3. Drizzle over salad and toss.

Tabbouleh (Parsley and Bulgur Salad)

Ingredients:

- ½ cup bulgur wheat, cooked
- 1 cup fresh parsley, finely chopped
- ½ cup cherry tomatoes, diced
- 2 green onions, chopped
- 2 tablespoons lemon juice
- 2 tablespoons olive oil
- ½ teaspoon salt

Instructions:

1. Mix bulgur, parsley, tomatoes, and green onions in a bowl.
2. Drizzle with lemon juice, olive oil, and salt.
3. Toss and serve.

Muhammara (Red Pepper and Walnut Dip)

Ingredients:

- 2 roasted red bell peppers
- ½ cup walnuts
- 1 tablespoon pomegranate molasses
- 1 tablespoon olive oil
- 1 teaspoon cumin
- ½ teaspoon salt

Instructions:

1. Blend roasted red peppers, walnuts, pomegranate molasses, olive oil, cumin, and salt.
2. Serve with pita bread.

Kibbeh (Stuffed Bulgur and Meat Croquettes)

Ingredients:

- 1 cup bulgur wheat
- ½ pound ground beef or lamb
- 1 small onion, chopped
- 1 teaspoon cinnamon
- 1 teaspoon allspice
- ½ teaspoon salt
- 1 tablespoon olive oil

Instructions:

1. Soak bulgur in water for 10 minutes, then drain.
2. Mix bulgur with ground meat, onion, cinnamon, allspice, and salt.
3. Shape into oval patties and fry in olive oil until golden brown.

Sfiha (Lebanese Meat Pies)

Ingredients:

- 2 cups all-purpose flour
- 1 teaspoon yeast
- ¾ cup warm water
- ½ teaspoon salt
- ½ pound ground beef or lamb
- 1 small onion, chopped
- ½ teaspoon cinnamon
- ½ teaspoon cumin
- 2 tablespoons pine nuts
- 1 tablespoon lemon juice

Instructions:

1. Mix flour, yeast, water, and salt to form a dough. Let rise for 1 hour.
2. Sauté ground meat with onion, cinnamon, cumin, pine nuts, and lemon juice.
3. Roll out dough into small circles and top with meat mixture.
4. Bake at 375°F (190°C) for 12–15 minutes.

Lamb Kofta Skewers

Ingredients:

- 1 lb ground lamb
- 1 small onion, grated
- 2 cloves garlic, minced
- 2 tablespoons fresh parsley, chopped
- 1 teaspoon ground cumin
- 1 teaspoon ground coriander
- ½ teaspoon cinnamon
- ½ teaspoon salt
- ½ teaspoon black pepper

Instructions:

1. Mix all ingredients in a bowl until well combined.
2. Shape the mixture around skewers into long sausage shapes.
3. Grill over medium heat for 10–12 minutes, turning occasionally.
4. Serve with pita bread and yogurt sauce.

Chicken Shawarma with Garlic Sauce

Ingredients:

- 2 boneless, skinless chicken thighs
- 2 tablespoons olive oil
- 1 teaspoon ground cumin
- 1 teaspoon paprika
- ½ teaspoon turmeric
- ½ teaspoon cinnamon
- ½ teaspoon salt
- ½ teaspoon black pepper
- Juice of 1 lemon

Garlic Sauce (Toum):

- 4 cloves garlic
- ½ cup olive oil
- 1 tablespoon lemon juice
- ¼ teaspoon salt

Instructions:

1. Mix chicken with olive oil, spices, and lemon juice. Marinate for at least 2 hours.
2. Grill or pan-fry chicken until fully cooked, about 6 minutes per side.
3. Blend garlic, olive oil, lemon juice, and salt until smooth.
4. Serve chicken with garlic sauce in pita bread.

Beef Kebab with Sumac Onions

Ingredients:

- 1 lb ground beef
- 1 small onion, grated
- 1 teaspoon ground cumin
- 1 teaspoon paprika
- ½ teaspoon sumac
- ½ teaspoon salt
- ½ teaspoon black pepper

Sumac Onions:

- 1 small red onion, thinly sliced
- 1 teaspoon sumac
- 1 teaspoon lemon juice
- 1 tablespoon chopped parsley

Instructions:

1. Mix beef with grated onion, spices, salt, and pepper. Shape into kebabs.
2. Grill over medium heat for 10–12 minutes, turning occasionally.
3. Toss sliced onions with sumac, lemon juice, and parsley.
4. Serve kebabs with sumac onions on flatbread.

Mujadara (Lentils and Rice with Caramelized Onions)

Ingredients:

- 1 cup lentils
- ½ cup basmati rice
- 2 large onions, thinly sliced
- 2 tablespoons olive oil
- 1 teaspoon cumin
- ½ teaspoon cinnamon
- ½ teaspoon salt

Instructions:

1. Cook lentils in water until tender, about 15 minutes. Drain.
2. Sauté onions in olive oil until deeply caramelized.
3. Add rice, cumin, cinnamon, and salt. Stir for 2 minutes.
4. Pour in 2 cups water, cover, and simmer for 15 minutes.
5. Stir in cooked lentils and fluff with a fork.

Koshari (Egyptian Lentil and Pasta Dish)

Ingredients:

- 1 cup cooked lentils
- 1 cup cooked rice
- 1 cup cooked pasta
- 1 small onion, thinly sliced
- 1 cup tomato sauce
- 1 teaspoon cumin
- 1 teaspoon vinegar
- ½ teaspoon chili flakes
- 2 tablespoons olive oil

Instructions:

1. Sauté onions in olive oil until crispy and golden brown. Set aside.
2. Heat tomato sauce with cumin, vinegar, and chili flakes. Simmer for 5 minutes.
3. Layer rice, pasta, and lentils in a bowl.
4. Top with tomato sauce and crispy onions.

Foul Medames (Fava Bean Stew)

Ingredients:

- 1 can fava beans, drained
- 1 clove garlic, minced
- 1 tablespoon lemon juice
- 1 tablespoon olive oil
- ½ teaspoon cumin
- ½ teaspoon salt
- Chopped parsley for garnish

Instructions:

1. Mash half of the fava beans and mix with the remaining beans.
2. Heat with garlic, lemon juice, olive oil, cumin, and salt.
3. Simmer for 5 minutes and garnish with parsley.

Stuffed Grape Leaves (Dolma)

Ingredients:

- 20 grape leaves, rinsed
- ½ cup cooked rice
- ½ cup ground lamb or beef (optional)
- 1 small onion, minced
- 1 teaspoon allspice
- ½ teaspoon cinnamon
- ½ teaspoon salt
- 1 tablespoon lemon juice

Instructions:

1. Mix rice, meat (if using), onion, spices, salt, and lemon juice.
2. Place a teaspoon of filling in each grape leaf and roll tightly.
3. Place in a pot, cover with water, and simmer for 30 minutes.

Makloubeh (Upside-Down Rice and Meat Dish)

Ingredients:

- 1 cup basmati rice
- ½ pound lamb or chicken, cubed
- 1 small eggplant, sliced
- 1 small potato, sliced
- 1 small onion, chopped
- 1 teaspoon cinnamon
- 1 teaspoon cumin
- ½ teaspoon salt
- 2 cups water

Instructions:

1. Sauté meat with onion, cumin, cinnamon, and salt. Cook until browned.
2. Fry eggplant and potatoes separately until golden.
3. Layer meat, eggplant, and potatoes in a pot.
4. Add rice and water. Cover and cook for 20 minutes.
5. Flip onto a plate before serving.

Samak Mashwi (Grilled Fish with Spices)

Ingredients:

- 2 whole fish (sea bass or snapper), cleaned
- 2 tablespoons olive oil
- 1 teaspoon cumin
- 1 teaspoon paprika
- ½ teaspoon salt
- ½ teaspoon black pepper
- Juice of 1 lemon

Instructions:

1. Rub fish with olive oil, spices, and lemon juice.
2. Grill over medium heat for 5–7 minutes per side.

Lebanese Garlic Toum Sauce

Ingredients:

- 4 cloves garlic
- ½ cup olive oil
- 1 tablespoon lemon juice
- ¼ teaspoon salt

Instructions:

1. Blend garlic, lemon juice, and salt until smooth.
2. Slowly drizzle in olive oil while blending until thick.

Harira (Moroccan Chickpea Soup)

Ingredients:

- 1 cup cooked chickpeas
- ½ cup lentils
- 1 small onion, diced
- 2 cloves garlic, minced
- 1 tomato, chopped
- 4 cups vegetable or chicken broth
- 1 teaspoon cumin
- ½ teaspoon cinnamon
- ½ teaspoon turmeric
- 1 tablespoon olive oil
- ¼ cup chopped cilantro

Instructions:

1. Heat olive oil in a pot and sauté onion and garlic.
2. Add tomatoes, chickpeas, lentils, broth, and spices.
3. Simmer for 25 minutes.
4. Garnish with fresh cilantro before serving.

Tahini and Date Energy Bites

Ingredients:

- 1 cup pitted dates
- ½ cup tahini
- ½ cup oats
- ¼ teaspoon cinnamon
- 2 tablespoons sesame seeds

Instructions:

1. Blend dates, tahini, oats, and cinnamon until combined.
2. Roll into small balls and coat with sesame seeds.
3. Refrigerate for at least 30 minutes.

Labneh with Olive Oil and Za'atar

Ingredients:

- 1 cup Greek yogurt
- 1 tablespoon olive oil
- 1 teaspoon za'atar
- ½ teaspoon salt

Instructions:

1. Strain Greek yogurt in a cheesecloth for 24 hours.
2. Transfer to a bowl and drizzle with olive oil.
3. Sprinkle with za'atar and salt before serving.

Roz Bel Laban (Creamy Rice Pudding)

Ingredients:

- ½ cup short-grain rice
- 2 cups milk
- ¼ cup sugar
- ½ teaspoon vanilla extract
- ½ teaspoon cinnamon
- 1 tablespoon crushed pistachios

Instructions:

1. Cook rice in milk over low heat until soft.
2. Stir in sugar and vanilla and simmer until thickened.
3. Garnish with cinnamon and pistachios.

Basbousa (Semolina Coconut Cake)

Ingredients:

- 1 cup semolina
- ½ cup shredded coconut
- ½ cup sugar
- ½ cup yogurt
- ½ teaspoon baking soda
- ½ teaspoon vanilla extract
- ½ cup syrup (sugar, water, lemon juice)

Instructions:

1. Mix semolina, coconut, sugar, yogurt, baking soda, and vanilla.
2. Pour into a greased pan and bake at 350°F (175°C) for 30 minutes.
3. Drizzle with syrup while warm.

Kunafa (Crispy Cheese and Syrup Dessert)

Ingredients:

- 2 cups shredded phyllo dough
- ½ cup melted butter
- 1 cup ricotta cheese
- ½ cup sugar syrup (sugar, water, lemon juice)
- ¼ cup crushed pistachios

Instructions:

1. Mix phyllo dough with melted butter and press half into a pan.
2. Spread ricotta cheese, then cover with remaining phyllo.
3. Bake at 375°F (190°C) for 30 minutes.
4. Drizzle with syrup and sprinkle with pistachios.

Baklava with Pistachios and Honey

Ingredients:

- 1 package phyllo dough
- 1 cup chopped pistachios
- ½ cup melted butter
- ½ cup honey
- ½ teaspoon cinnamon

Instructions:

1. Layer phyllo dough, brushing each layer with butter.
2. Spread pistachios and cinnamon after every few layers.
3. Bake at 350°F (175°C) for 35 minutes.
4. Drizzle with honey before serving.

Atayef (Stuffed Pancakes with Nuts or Cream)

Ingredients:

- 1 cup flour
- 1 teaspoon baking powder
- 1 cup milk
- 1 teaspoon sugar
- ½ cup crushed walnuts or ricotta cheese

Instructions:

1. Mix flour, baking powder, milk, and sugar into a batter.
2. Cook small pancakes on one side only.
3. Fill with walnuts or ricotta, then fold and seal.

Maamoul (Date-Filled Shortbread Cookies)

Ingredients:

- 2 cups semolina flour
- ½ cup butter
- ½ cup sugar
- ½ teaspoon cinnamon
- 1 cup pitted dates, mashed

Instructions:

1. Mix semolina, butter, sugar, and cinnamon into a dough.
2. Fill with mashed dates and shape into small cookies.
3. Bake at 350°F (175°C) for 20 minutes.

Qatayef Asafiri (Mini Pancakes with Cream)

Ingredients:

- 1 cup flour
- 1 teaspoon baking powder
- 1 cup milk
- 1 teaspoon sugar
- ½ cup ashta (clotted cream)
- ¼ cup crushed pistachios
- 1 tablespoon honey

Instructions:

1. Mix flour, baking powder, milk, and sugar into a batter.
2. Cook small pancakes on one side only.
3. Fill with ashta, fold, and garnish with pistachios and honey.

Halva (Sweet Sesame Paste Dessert)

Ingredients:

- 1 cup tahini
- ½ cup honey
- ½ teaspoon vanilla extract
- ¼ cup chopped pistachios

Instructions:

1. Mix tahini, honey, and vanilla until thick.
2. Spread into a dish and press with pistachios.
3. Chill for 1 hour before serving.

Cardamom and Saffron Rice Pudding

Ingredients:

- ½ cup short-grain rice
- 2 cups milk
- ¼ cup sugar
- ½ teaspoon ground cardamom
- 1 pinch saffron threads, soaked in 1 tablespoon warm milk
- 1 teaspoon rose water (optional)
- 2 tablespoons crushed pistachios

Instructions:

1. Cook rice in milk over low heat until soft.
2. Stir in sugar, cardamom, saffron milk, and rose water.
3. Simmer until thickened.
4. Garnish with crushed pistachios.

Persian Love Cake with Rose Water

Ingredients:

- 1 cup almond flour
- 1 cup all-purpose flour
- ½ cup sugar
- ½ teaspoon cardamom
- ½ teaspoon baking powder
- ½ cup melted butter
- 2 eggs
- 2 tablespoons rose water
- ¼ cup chopped pistachios

Instructions:

1. Preheat oven to 350°F (175°C).
2. Mix dry ingredients, then add butter, eggs, and rose water.
3. Pour batter into a greased cake pan.
4. Bake for 30–35 minutes.
5. Garnish with pistachios.

Turkish Delight with Pistachios

Ingredients:

- 2 cups sugar
- 1 cup water
- ½ teaspoon lemon juice
- ½ teaspoon rose water
- ½ cup cornstarch
- ½ cup pistachios, chopped
- Powdered sugar for dusting

Instructions:

1. Boil sugar, water, and lemon juice until syrupy.
2. Mix cornstarch with water, then add to syrup.
3. Cook until thick and smooth.
4. Stir in rose water and pistachios.
5. Pour into a greased pan and cool.
6. Cut into squares and dust with powdered sugar.

Pomegranate Molasses Chicken

Ingredients:

- 2 boneless, skinless chicken breasts
- 2 tablespoons pomegranate molasses
- 1 tablespoon olive oil
- 1 teaspoon cumin
- ½ teaspoon paprika
- ½ teaspoon salt
- ½ teaspoon black pepper

Instructions:

1. Mix pomegranate molasses, olive oil, and spices.
2. Marinate chicken for at least 30 minutes.
3. Grill or bake at 375°F (190°C) for 20 minutes.

Bamia (Okra and Tomato Stew)

Ingredients:

- 2 cups fresh okra, trimmed
- 1 small onion, diced
- 2 cloves garlic, minced
- 1 can diced tomatoes
- 1 teaspoon cumin
- ½ teaspoon cinnamon
- 1 tablespoon olive oil
- 1 teaspoon lemon juice

Instructions:

1. Sauté onion and garlic in olive oil.
2. Add okra, tomatoes, cumin, cinnamon, and lemon juice.
3. Simmer for 20 minutes.

Fasolia (White Bean and Tomato Stew)

Ingredients:

- 1 can white beans, drained
- 1 small onion, chopped
- 2 cloves garlic, minced
- 1 cup tomato sauce
- 1 teaspoon cumin
- ½ teaspoon paprika
- 1 tablespoon olive oil

Instructions:

1. Sauté onion and garlic in olive oil.
2. Add beans, tomato sauce, and spices.
3. Simmer for 15 minutes.

Moroccan Spiced Carrot Salad

Ingredients:

- 2 cups carrots, grated
- 1 teaspoon cumin
- ½ teaspoon cinnamon
- 1 tablespoon lemon juice
- 1 tablespoon olive oil
- ¼ cup chopped fresh parsley

Instructions:

1. Toss carrots with cumin, cinnamon, lemon juice, and olive oil.
2. Sprinkle with fresh parsley.

Dukkah-Crusted Roasted Vegetables

Ingredients:

- 1 zucchini, sliced
- 1 red bell pepper, chopped
- 1 cup cauliflower florets
- 2 tablespoons dukkah spice mix
- 1 tablespoon olive oil

Instructions:

1. Toss vegetables with dukkah and olive oil.
2. Roast at 400°F (200°C) for 20 minutes.

Feta and Olive Mezze Platter

Ingredients:

- ½ cup feta cheese, cubed
- ½ cup mixed olives
- 1 tablespoon olive oil
- 1 teaspoon oregano
- ½ teaspoon red pepper flakes

Instructions:

1. Toss feta and olives with olive oil, oregano, and red pepper flakes.

Grilled Halloumi with Honey and Nuts

Ingredients:

- 4 slices halloumi cheese
- 1 tablespoon honey
- 2 tablespoons chopped walnuts

Instructions:

1. Grill halloumi for 2 minutes per side.
2. Drizzle with honey and top with walnuts.

Shish Taouk (Middle Eastern Chicken Skewers)

Ingredients:

- 1 lb boneless chicken breast, cubed
- 2 tablespoons yogurt
- 1 tablespoon lemon juice
- 1 tablespoon olive oil
- 2 cloves garlic, minced
- 1 teaspoon paprika
- 1 teaspoon cumin
- ½ teaspoon turmeric
- ½ teaspoon salt
- ½ teaspoon black pepper

Instructions:

1. Mix yogurt, lemon juice, olive oil, garlic, and spices in a bowl.
2. Marinate chicken in the mixture for at least 2 hours.
3. Thread chicken onto skewers and grill for 10–12 minutes, turning occasionally.

Spiced Lentil Soup with Cumin and Coriander

Ingredients:

- 1 cup red lentils
- 1 small onion, diced
- 2 cloves garlic, minced
- 1 teaspoon cumin
- 1 teaspoon coriander
- ½ teaspoon turmeric
- 4 cups vegetable broth
- 1 tablespoon olive oil
- Lemon wedges for serving

Instructions:

1. Heat olive oil in a pot and sauté onion and garlic.
2. Add lentils, spices, and broth. Simmer for 20 minutes.
3. Blend until smooth and serve with lemon wedges.

Batata Harra (Spicy Lebanese Potatoes)

Ingredients:

- 2 large potatoes, cubed
- 2 tablespoons olive oil
- 1 teaspoon paprika
- ½ teaspoon chili flakes
- 2 cloves garlic, minced
- ¼ cup fresh cilantro, chopped
- ½ teaspoon salt

Instructions:

1. Toss potatoes with olive oil, paprika, chili flakes, and salt.
2. Roast at 400°F (200°C) for 25 minutes.
3. Sauté garlic in olive oil, add roasted potatoes, and toss with cilantro.

Warak Enab (Grape Leaves Stuffed with Rice and Meat)

Ingredients:

- 20 grape leaves, rinsed
- ½ cup uncooked rice
- ½ cup ground beef or lamb
- 1 small onion, minced
- 1 teaspoon allspice
- ½ teaspoon cinnamon
- ½ teaspoon salt
- 1 tablespoon lemon juice

Instructions:

1. Mix rice, meat, onion, spices, and lemon juice.
2. Place 1 teaspoon of filling in each grape leaf and roll tightly.
3. Place in a pot, cover with water, and simmer for 40 minutes.

Arayes (Stuffed Pita with Spiced Meat)

Ingredients:

- 2 pita breads, halved
- ½ lb ground beef or lamb
- 1 small onion, minced
- 1 teaspoon cumin
- 1 teaspoon paprika
- ½ teaspoon salt
- ½ teaspoon black pepper
- 1 tablespoon olive oil

Instructions:

1. Mix ground meat with onion, cumin, paprika, salt, and pepper.
2. Stuff mixture into pita halves.
3. Brush with olive oil and grill for 5 minutes per side.

Sahlab (Warm Milk and Orchid Powder Drink)

Ingredients:

- 2 cups milk
- 1 tablespoon cornstarch (or sahlab powder)
- 1 tablespoon sugar
- ½ teaspoon cinnamon
- 1 teaspoon rose water
- 1 tablespoon crushed pistachios

Instructions:

1. Dissolve cornstarch in a little cold milk.
2. Heat remaining milk and sugar, then stir in cornstarch mixture.
3. Simmer until thickened, then add rose water.
4. Garnish with cinnamon and pistachios.

Rosewater Lemonade with Mint

Ingredients:

- 2 cups water
- ½ cup lemon juice
- ¼ cup sugar
- 1 teaspoon rosewater
- ½ cup fresh mint leaves
- Ice cubes

Instructions:

1. Stir lemon juice, water, sugar, and rosewater until sugar dissolves.
2. Add mint leaves and let steep for 10 minutes.
3. Serve over ice.

Turkish Coffee with Cardamom

Ingredients:

- 1 cup water
- 1 tablespoon finely ground Turkish coffee
- ¼ teaspoon ground cardamom
- 1 teaspoon sugar (optional)

Instructions:

1. Add water, coffee, and cardamom to a cezve (Turkish coffee pot).
2. Heat slowly, stirring once. Do not let it boil.
3. Pour into small cups and let the grounds settle before drinking.

Mint Tea with Pine Nuts

Ingredients:

- 2 cups hot water
- 2 teaspoons loose-leaf black tea
- ¼ cup fresh mint leaves
- 1 teaspoon sugar (optional)
- 1 tablespoon pine nuts

Instructions:

1. Steep tea leaves in hot water for 5 minutes.
2. Add mint leaves and sugar, let steep for 2 more minutes.
3. Serve with pine nuts in the cup.